D0367080

DUANE NIATUM

Drawings of the Song Animals:

NEW AND SELECTED POEMS

HOLY COW! PRESS • 1991
DULUTH, MINNESOTA

Library of Congress Cataloging-in-Publication Data
Niatum, Duane, 1938-
        Drawings of the song animals: new and selected poems / Duane Niatum.
        p.   cm.
        ISBN 0-930100-43-3 (cloth) : $18.95. — ISBN 0-930100-44-1 (pbk.) : $10.95
        I. Title
        PS3564.I17D7 1991
        811'.54—dc20   90-82294
                                                                  CIP

Publisher's Address: Distributor's Address:
Holy Cow! Press   The Talman Company, Inc.
Post Office Box 3170   150 Fifth Avenue
Mount Royal Station   New York, New York 10011
Duluth, Minnesota 55803

This project is supported, in part, by a grant from the National Endowment for the
Arts in Washington, D.C., a Federal Agency.

Contents

Digging Out the Roots

Songs for the Harvester of Dreams

New Poems

Author's Preface

In making this selection from over twenty-five years of work, I have chosen only fifteen poems from each of the first four books. It is my belief that it takes a long time to discover what your art is all about, and the years have proven this early conviction to be true. Artists of every field need time to experiment, fail, and occasionally, succeed. Besides, the years have shown Paul Valéry correct when he warned, "a poem is never finished, it is only abandoned."

Along with the loss of faith in the early efforts, the younger selves in these reject poems mirror strangers because the years piling up have rearranged my memories. So I disown much of my early efforts as well as early selves. When William Meredith chose his selected poems he left out several because he could hear the voice of an impersonator. I, too, omitted poems where Raven or Coyote had played tricks with my music. Thus, the poems included may not always be the best from the past, but they somehow still retain the voice I feel is mine.

Since art is an attempt to engage in the mysteries of life, I make every effort to continue learning and expanding my possibilities. As Auden pointed out in *The Dyer's Hand*, the best poetry in English from the beginning to today, attempts to capture the voice we hear in everyday speech. With the voice of people in the home and on the street, I feel a real social atmosphere is woven throughout the work, and not some aesthetic dross. The social and aesthetic traditions of my Native American ancestors have merely reinforced this point of view.

An author's chronological account of his work, like the selected poems offered here, insinuates an autobiography or at least a character that he would like the reader to accept: that of a candid man paying close attention to the events, dreams, and aspirations of his life—to give significance to the few multi-faceted experiences he can transform into art. An ideal that is seldom achieved. Yet I accept the failure: too much happens that one leaves out of one's work for an accurate portrayal.

My four books record with joy a few human and spiritual encounters that I don't want to ignore. I'm happy the books have the associations they do. *After the Death of an Elder Klallam* paid tribute to my native American heritage, both family and other, and was dedicated to Ted Roethke, one of America's greatest poets. I had the good fortune to visit his poetry workshop at the University of Washington in 1961. His poetry and prose and this exposure and Nelson Bentley's evening workshop at the same university directed me to the right lyrical road.

Ascending Red Cedar Moon was dedicated to some special women in my life and our elder poets, my mentors, if you will: too many to name. They are honored by my efforts to learn how to fly with their words, make them a part of my own verbal textures. As Possum Eliot let it be known, "immature poets borrow, mature poets steal." *Digging Out The Roots* was dedicated to the small tribe of my friends, I'm still humbled by those friends that remain. *Songs For The Harvester of Dreams* was dedicated to my son, Marc, and the Children of the First Americans. The new poems in the last section have not previously appeared in a book. May they show a new direction, a new departure from the dream wheel's center.

—Duane Niatum
Seattle, Washington
May, 1988

In memory of Young and Lucy Patsy,
my maternal Great Grandparents

After the Death of an Elder Klallam

1970

PORTRAIT ❧

With eyes the color of dark-brown mushrooms,
peering from an oval cranium,
cheeks thin and Salish high,
sling-shot tucked away in back-pocket,
his mind runs for the road to the woods.
He decides to skip school to watch
a heron scan the shallows at Chimacum Creek,
center its return under its wing,
evade the eyes of any observer.

His hair, combed by the sun, is brushed black
by the ferns and wind. The mouth,
two parallel lines, curves upside down.
It has said the wrong thing at the wrong time,
but occasionally stays closed beneath the stars.
When confronted with America's tourists,
he frowns, a Klallam with reservations,
then smiles when he tells of the night
he stole the sheriff's crêpe-blue
station wagon with silver-sequined daughter
giggling beside him at the wheel.

Grandson to hawk and cedar, he drinks
with deer and dragonfly at the pool,
a slow dancer on the thundering ground.
Stopping to collect the scattered songs,
he grows in the shade of mountain ash,
sea swirls, fish, love and its illusions,
nature left, nature imagined.

Out of the dream this creature leaves
the field counting the steps across the water,
taking him deep into its turnings.

OLD TILLICUM ❧
for Francis Patsy, my grandfather

A timber blue haze dissolves
on chokecherry leaves, thimbleberry, and the ants'
footprints at the beginning of the thicket.
Pebbles in the water leap before the salmon
in the current; the brush keeps us guessing
at the steps of the elk kicking dirt
on its run down the canyon.
The sky lifts my alder-smoked frame
like an unbroken impulse of the mountain,
Memp-ch-ton, to pause with goldenrod, willow,
and blue jay flying across the river of my people.

An old Klallam, I sit with my grandson
while from the fern distances the Elwha rushes
seaward. I watch for the voices
of the river to show him the currents to manhood,
strengthen his green awkwardness,
flush his cheek with spruce light,
and promise my brittle bones a few more moons.

First mountain to choose his ancestors,
mirrored in the rapids and the falling sun,
it dwarfs the white firs that once spread
the village fires like a family of sap and lichen.
Pitch-dry with age I am here
to see that my daughter's son starts
the long journey back to the clearing of Old Patsy,
sings for me the story of when Old Patsy
pulled in a net swimming with herring,

the net that will pull him on like the tide.
As a boy once frightened of the surf's
crack below the hemlock, pine, and cedar,
our evening walks by lantern to the circle
and home of Young and Lucy Patsy,
he now disappears beyond the edge
of the mountain's sunset; a fox running shadows.

By the time the quail roost and the dusk
is mute on the ridge above the ravine,
I tell him of the legend of the seven brothers
that named the village long burned to ash,
how these ancestors danced into the fire
to forget. And like their totem to the Thunderbird,
the moon drifts full height into the next horizon,
returning it to its birth.

Perhaps asking us all to touch the earth
from this dawn to the next on through summer,
it looks as if his guardian spirit
is answering his chant to let him carry home
for good what the water drum has offered.

As his grandfather I rise too late
to return home with little crow. Instead, I hear
his first jump through chance's hoop.

VALLEY OF THE SPIRITS 🔥

Talking to the remnants,
the old one rattles the ground,
naming the wound singers:
raven, with one toe hooked to a pine branch,
another, snapping back at the fire;
owl, with one eye on the eyeless moon,
the other on the slope with a thousand daisy eyes.

The old man says the whalers'
village beyond the mountain once lit
the dream ashes, shared the tracks.
And somewhere on its crust pain
roams in search of its lost echo,
a host, while a dragonfly nearby,
hovers above the witch flowing

in the moss-crescent lake.
This slime-drenched creature polarizes
us with eyes that open and close
like angry flies the leanest trout refuse.
Dancing toward another ghost,
the old man greets his ancestor,
a bird whose screech thunders

through each moving thing beneath
cliff and cave. His story's
downbeat is that if we are humble
this bird might give us a storm,
a new path of singing bones,

a meadow of sea-bleached stars.
As the sun passes trillium and frog,
enters the crack of its own division,
the elder points to the valley's end.
It lies open like a shell on the sand.

TO MY COAST SALISH ANCESTORS

In the late evening, rain and fog.
Who sends dancers with elk-teeth rattles
to roam the alley next to my cottage?
Their song enters the window,
a Swinomish chorus: each step
that brings them closer forms
another mask of the moon,

another color of the Northwest sea.
I open the door and follow;
they toss legends I must find in the dark.
In their honor I cross knives with them;
our union is a force the wind receives.
I am of this coast and its keeper.

OLD WOMAN AWAITING THE
GREYHOUND BUS

Almost singing, she stares past the crowd and flies.
Wearing a black-knit shawl that fed
generations of moths, warmed the small bodies
of many grandchildren, her face wrinkles
into a smiling heap of eggshells.
Seeing me watching her, she asks me to sit down,
her baroque cane pinning our age to the floor
like an icon. I see those grandchildren
in her eyes do figure eights on thin ice,
flood her dreaming with forgotten jokes.

Her smile fades to an apple left to brown
on a bedroom table four generations asleep,
and in blue humility, free of remembrances,
she drops her teeth into the grave of appearances
at the bottom of her purse,
now somewhere in a room of yellow voices.

No longer caring about the odds in her age,
she breathes with the apple peasants of the world,
and chews time like a white rabbit.

RAVEN

The old ones whose fathers hunted
the whale boast to the children
half listening of the chase they heard
when young, before a dog salmon fire,
but the last canoe to skim the waves hangs
from the roof of the general store,
a relic dangling in obtuse space,
its myths as white as the storekeeper

who bought it for the tourists.
Even he knows few survive the advance
of steel and concrete, rust and spores,
and if the Great Spirit ever spoke, it
must have been before his father or theirs.
Trapped in an ignorance he cannot fathom,
he watches for the owl they claim will
pick his bones as clean as the wind on the sea.

He sits down to drink with the elders
and chatters back to the chipmunk
racing across the woodpile for the night.
When silence consumes its chant,
Killer whale leaps near the river's mouth,
pounds the beach to a raven's caw.
With Snowberry woman but a photograph
in the window, the stories of mornings

elk, cougar, and beaver were seen
drinking the green dew of the Hoko

with insects, glimmer only
in the light of the ashes.
Now the crier bearing the new season
to the village is the slow beat of the rain.
But once, when this rain turned to snow,
the snow to feathers, a voice rose

with a storm to sting the whalers:
"I am Kwatee, the Changer, your friend."
Fog Dreamer, the eldest singer, shook his
head and threw his rattle at the creature:
"You're too late, our children have fled."
He spit on the creature's black toes;
looked long at the mud slide of the longhouse.
Kwatee, alone, beat huge wings to stars.

Then like cones splitting from the pine,
the old ones staggered off to sleep.
Raven might have watched them fall,
Killer whale dive to the shadowless sky
when the fire cooled to coal.

THE MAN FROM HADLOCK &

He was called Old Cedar,
a storyteller to forget, not believe—
spoke to beaver, wolf, and bear,
along the many paths through the forest.
Some people claimed his eye
followed the moon too closely,
rested his bones too near the snail's,
slept in the hollows of night
wearing raven's birth mask.

His neighbors avoided him because
he would go and dance all night
on Skunk Island, sleep there,
and never get poison oak or ivy.
They were sure his song of the Hoko river
brought the bats and the rain.
From the beginning they hated
his stories of the Changer:
eagle, fox, and blue jay.

They feared he had some
mysterious hold on their children
who stole away to his longhouse
to laugh and sing his willow songs.
Who but he lived
in Thunderbird's ashes
and could pull salmon
from the deepest, blackest currents?
Then one sunrise he chanted

to those around the fire of love,
courage and death. Since he
had long ignored the parents who
chased him time and again
with sticks, he spread a fog
of patience over his small friends,
his voice slowing down to whispers,
and greeted the owl with a keen
that kept each child in his shadow
floating toward the window,
the river rocks and rapids.

VISITING MY SON MARC AT PORT ANGELES ❧

I

The mountain keeping this town in evergreens
is shaped by the tide, drifting man
into the flat view of the flounder,
hair seal, the clown shadow for oyster and blue crab,
madrona, the storm crier for smelt.

The town works as calmly as the morning,
unmoved by the strangers trading dreams.
Here Marc lives with his mother,
near the forest where my mother's family
heard alpine frogs on the wind,
and if his mother lets him return
to the Klallam mountain, he may step
like the cougar across glacial trails,
proud, silent, ready to roam by himself,
to sit before the fire as First People
name the way to their longhouse.

He might yet dig for the heartbeat in the ashes,
choose to drum for shaman and salmon.
Maybe one day he'll reach shallow water
like my pathfinder, the great blue heron,
although not quite six winters.

II

November air is the day's brisk teacher.
Listening to mallards, sandpipers, and herring gulls
gossip like women picking blueberries,

we wander the waterfront piers,
almost reach the coast in the ships
gliding from port in the snow-paddle sun.

Settled in the waves salt-edge, he runs down
the pier to count the rhythms
of the Strait of Juan de Fuca,
slow my heart to a kingfisher's.
I skip a clam shell on the water to harvest the joy.

He stares into the singing wave,
his concentration leaves me short of breath,
reflects the breaker's white wingtip,
the dolphins' surge through the catacombs of his blood.

III

My grandfather joins us at the apex of our journey
as Marc gazes at the ebb and flow.
This elder appears as a mask
shining through my son's face
despite having died many moons before his birth.
The colors and lines on his seventy-three year-
old face reveal legend and path we can season in.
Then retreating on the out-going tide
like his grandfather, Old Patsy,
chief of the Hadlock clan,
my oldest friend points to my son
laughing at the mud hens
surfacing from underneath the pier.

TWO BEARS AND THE TIDE ❧

Another car slows to a stop,
scares the dogs
that dash for cover
behind the longhouse.
Two Bears seems bent in a trap
of rage that sees
no way to drive
the featherless away,

back to the cities, convince
them before it is
permanent, that a mind
running in the ruins,
digging for the vision
of other people's dreams
will fail to find a home,
a refuge from shadows

or what they fled, for the beach
at La Push has no place
to hang their broken mirrors,
words, fragmented and off-key.
Thus he bolts like the deer
as the swarm grows steady,
moves in on family and village,
swirling hawk and child into one

tangle, knotted and unraveled
as a blanket of cinders.

He refuses to believe
the fire is burned out,
his brothers are not
throwing nets to dry,
that cane, harpoon,
Killer Whale and Raven

have disappeared from the smokehouse,
from the shadow dancing down
the night, chanting to dawn.
Keeper of the color wheel,
Two Bears opens the flap
to the sweatlodge, prepares
to cleanse himself of loss,
the morning walks in mist,

his ancestral wind songs,
the cormorant's cry—*garoo, garoo*
that light the shells on tomorrow.
He sits before the stones
to talk with the animal
that will cover the road
with snow, shield what is left.
When the creature leaps

through the circle forming
from the trail of steam,
the rain will twist
to ice in the cities.

ON HEARING A MARSH BIRD SPEAK OF
OLD PATSY'S CLAN ❧

for William Stafford

I

Since they had many feasts on this beach
facing the red willow shadows of Memp-ch-ton,
I dig for their arrowheads and rattles
pared from red cedar and yew tree earth.
The buried voices of Hadlock village still answer
the deer climbing the trail of sunset,
ride the waves like the whale from the coast,
shake like peace poles undulating the wind
that ends at the longhouse.

Old Patsy's grandson told me there are
countless ways to listen to the bones:
to start is to strip naked,
bend to face the moon covering the Elwha river,
let the current be your blood's.

II

My mind rises and glides beyond the forest,
a raven passing over the graves' black mirrors.
The first layer calls for a long drive under water,
the second count the salmon's heart as your compass,
the third run for the flying music
and return like the wolf.

III

Hadlock elders resisted the invasion
by living behind the totem crest of Thunderbird,
dancing each potlatch until they dropped.
I watch Chief Old Patsy and Chetzemoka,
Leschi, Sealth, and Joseph retire
into the longhouse of the Shadow People
without desire for suicide or defeat.
These men teach me every hoop
to eat the rain and mushrooms so I can
dance with the dead until our breaths are stone,
when the First Salmon People flash in my eyes,
nourish my one syllable of faith
like the loon's cry.

IV

The last dawn lays a basket of oysters on the fire:
never knife the animals in your soul,
the butterflies in your storms,
stand like your grandfathers on this Salish ground
where shamans gave our darkness to the stars.

ELEGY FOR CHIEF SEALTH (1786-1866)

The white man will never be alone.
Let him be just and deal kindly with my people,
for the dead are not powerless.

Compromised by sorrow,
you embrace the winter rains
at the edge of the diminished forest,
your face a leather sheet
of salt winds from the Sound inlets,
the sacred camas islands of your fathers,
and chant of eighty moons turning to dust.

Because the guardian spirits
coot all year of the white man's flood
from the Eastern seaboard,
you hear Death's call to burn alone
in the fire of the black sun.
The waves of ships, covered wagons,
broke your arrows, pierced your shield,
shot the eagle from your sky.
And screams for Alaska gold
paralyzed your children for generations.

Yet, as if drumbeats rising
to cover the rocks far from shore,
those first Duwamish dancers with feet
the colors of daybreak, the remaining
tribes regain a part of the soil;
leave your children a small joy,
the glimpse of a heron, shifting in the reeds.

YE OLD CURIOSITY SHOP ❧

Even more grotesque than a laundromat,
the stains of a pawnshop window,
its shopkeepers are the unacknowledged
joke sticks of trickster.
Their weasel smiles pun Seattle like skid road.
Outside the entrance a cigar-store Indian,
with the entombed stare of a museum sculpture,
draws the tourists from the East
for the last time into the damp snare
of seashore ornaments and trinkets
for manufactured bores.
With the forest side-step of a crow,
the black eyes of a shaker, he
abandons the city of red rain and dives
into the water at the end of the pier.

AFTER THE DEATH OF AN ELDER KLALLAM ❦

I

Great-uncle Joe sat with a bottle of beer
in one hand and a steaming mussel in the other,
chanting under the Moon of Dry Grass,
the story of Kwatee, the Changer.
His grandchildren and his brother's huddled,
awed by his heavy-cedared frame and shadow,
painted in the sand by the fire.
When his laughter cracked with the pine logs
that smelled of kelp and seaweed, we saw
the Thunderbird surface before the whale.

Twelve years have passed the Hadlock flats
since I last saw his fishnets hanging
through winter across the common stream.
What blizzard afternoon was it
he pantomimed the gait of the black elk
who was only seen by the Trickster;
and the Chinook salmon held in a net,
and because of his copper eyes and flapping
defiance, he thew it back into the sea?
Oh when did the magic of a whale hunt
darken to nothing more than wish?

I can still hear his obscene shouts to the crows
the morning he slipped on a crab shell mound,
almost failing to toss feast bones
to the Herring People.

II

Today, serviceberry and nettle hide his home
and my grandfather's that was across the road.
And the driftwood animals he carved
for the entrance to Old Patsy's longhouse
mirror the rainbow spirits of his grandchildren.

So what are we to make of the blue spruce
without you, grand-uncle? Who else
besides your brother and sister, father and mother,
saw the forest breathe when the red-breasted
woodpecker was silent? How long before
the Hadlock village of Old Patsy and Lach-ka-nim
vanished like the sands under a wave
did you and your family break apart?
Was it when your father's father and family
were forced to leave Hadlock Bay
to live on the Skokomish reservation,
the reservation the family kept escaping?
Or was it your son Michael's death,
your brother Francis'?

Now my generation lies stripped to our hides,
charred saplings, the youngest roots
in the soil of many seasons.

III

In the wind of audible branches I return
the song of the yew tree shield,
as my great-uncle did when the sea called
him back to live with oyster and starfish,
soothe the hunger of cod and crab.
When he waved to us for the last celebration
in the amber silence, the salmon
were weaving through the dark rapids
of sapphire to spawn in Chimacum Creek.

On visiting Seabeck, his birthplace
and my grandfather's, where in his youth
he drummed the green moon to rise,
the clan of the dead, the totem fishermen
and singers, closed my eyes to the blood's pulse.

IV

Brother to chickadee and wolf,
raven and kingfisher, deer and cougar,
rain soaked and restless,
I hold to the ground of these cedarmen,
the earth shifting and sliding beneath my feet,
continue digging for the dream wheel
of my great-uncle, Joseph, elder to Thunderbird,
hawk, and sparrow.

MIXED MEDIA ❧

The stars grow lemon
in the field, spread
like tea leaves in
a cup; red-wing
blackbirds fold themselves
into the fence,
corn dreamers.

The sky undulating
with clouds returns
gold-throated arpeggios
to the one walking
at sunrise, sunfall.

Light as the air
I sit on my
cottage steps;
a tom cat come
home to die for
the day.

A TRIBUTE TO CHIEF JOSEPH (1840?-1904) ఌ

Never reaching the promised land in Canada,
HIN-MAH-TOO-YAH-LAT-KET:
"Thunder-rolling-in-the-mountains,"
the fugitive chief sits in a corner
of the prison car headed for Oklahoma,
chained to his warriors,
a featherless hawk in exile.

He sees out the window
geese rise from the storm's center
and knows more men died
by snow blizzard ·
than by cavalry shot.

Still his father's shield
of Wallowa Valley deer and elk
flashes in his eyes
and coyote runs the circles
and a cricket swallows the dark.

How many songs this elder
sang to break the cycle
of cold weather and disease
his people coughed and breathed
in this land of drifting ice.

Now sleepless as the door-guard,
the train rattles like dirt in his teeth,
straw in his eyes.

Holding rage in the palm of his fist,
his people's future spirals to red-forest dust,
leaves his bones on the track,
his soul in the whistle.

Ascending Red Cedar Moon

1974

COAST SALISH ROCK OFF
BAINBRIDGE ISLAND ❧

for Mary Randlett

I

He tosses a pail of water across the face
to see deeper into the longhouse eyes
of the oldest ancestor of his language,

touch each birth-scar of the family,
listen to the order of sand and yellow cedar,
sockeye and fishnet, sea rose and oyster,

gulls skimming the whitecaps,
the green and blue path of the sculpin,
singing fish who lives under the boulders,

time drinking up the season,
sapping spring air as unassuming
as the red-breasted woodpecker.

II

On hearing the tap, tap, tap bird spring
from one dead tree to the next stump,
down the shore from where the rock divides

the light in almost the same dance patterns
as the great blue heron in the cattails,
on one leg to outwit the minnow's tide tricks,

somehow the rock chants the legend
of every village fire around Puget Sound

only as dead as the tracks of the porcupine sun,
where paddles still seem to thrust themselves
into canoe charms, ravens' chatter
about the killer whales' dorsal fins

cutting through the moon-troughs.

III

So when the long-leaf rains broke
the clouds into whirling branches and chilled
his nerves with a gale, bent him like a reed,

his direction back to the cottage,
drive to the city with drums thundering
in the four directions, he knew by dawn
to sing each winter of water and of stone.

CHIEF LESCHI OF THE NISQUALLY ❧

He awoke this morning uneasily from a dream;
Thunderbird had crashed through
the jail wall like a club.
And from its circle, Nisqually women

led him back to their river, the dance of its song.
For a few changes in the wind
he burned in the forest like a red cedar,
his branches fanning blue flames
toward the white men taking the camas valley
for their pigs and cows.
Musing over wolf tracks, the offspring of snow,
the memory of his wives and children
keeps him mute. Flickering in the dawn embers,
his faith grows grizzly, tricks the soldiers
like a fawn, sleeping as the brush.
The soldiers make jokes about his fate,
frozen as a bat against their throat.
Still, death will take him

only to his father's burial mound,
past the rope's sinewy snap.
The bars lock in but his tired body; he will
eat little and speak less before he hangs.

NO ONE REMEMBERS THE VILLAGE OF WHITE FIR 🦎

I

As a child of red and yellow cedar, hemlock,
and the sea, I often slept under totem and star,
hanging from the ceiling of a black cave
like a bat to muffle the drone of my mother's
wrath that followed me here.

Time formed itself with Elwha rhymes,
the rainbow river of my ancestors,
whose art was carving, weaving, fishing,
hunting, dance, and occasionally war.
The wind then clacked like a raven rattle,
shaking alpine meters from the dark.
Salmon people swam the rapid dreams of children
playing with the blue jay and chipmunk.
And when my grandfather died in my youth,
I sealed off his path to the mountain
like a cave.

II

Three steps from the eagle's nest, my blood soared.
The splash and whirl of the river in the morning
was like a heartbeat rolling from the sky.
Reaching the snow tip of Memp-ch-ton,
the white wing of its summit,
wild rose and lupine
rooted to the breaks in stone.

On some days I ran through a childhood
of a dozen myths, saw the fruit

on the chokecherry tree ripen in the light
of the Moon of Dry Grass.
I plucked those memories for my escape
from the wreckage of scars.

III

I crawled deeper into the cave,
inching my way from the nightmare.
I was furless, a grizzly bear clawing my way,
out of the hissing, howling blizzard.
Seatco chased me to the edge of my cries;
Raven tossed me into skunk's arms.

My grandfather appeared in the passage,
sadly shaking his head, shamed by my fear
but not my failure. Grandfather,
you and Great Uncle and your father were
the only men I have known: your spirits
have been by shield. Someday, may I
face the storm with courage, offer
your songs to the children, our elders,
and the nameless poor?

IV

Figures woven into the baskets' sides
work quietly through the morning;
and the women who collected the bear grass
and cedar bark for weaving are always

the first to see the sun reach the river.
Offering to live out his story,
an elder walks with the stars one last night,
watches wrens eat blackberries.

v

Spinning on the colors of the meadow,
the earth covers up her tracks
with a celebration of acorn and honeybee.
The women picking camas roots tease the children.
Yet today the old paths are harder
to find like the eagle, deer, and fern pickers.
And the eroding forest barely draws
the stranger into the clearing,
the red-bone center of sunrise.

VI

I watch for the shifts in the orange fire,
seek the glow of cedar cones in ash,
to burn in the city, until the face
of my grandfather smiles before vanishing
in the rainbow. Never quite as constant
as the moon, I speak to the bats again—
stop when old Trickster beak calls

      "Niatum!   Niatum!"

ON LEAVING BALTIMORE ❧

I

Memory is as pale as the face on the moon,
as destitute and as pocked. I shed
it like a skin. But it is silence
that opens the window, the mirror, the door.
Condemning me to the teeth,
it pushes me into the street everyone
has heard tear the owl from the oak,
scanning the field that remains.

II

A falling star heaves a few words against
the wall: it's over, it's over, it's over.
Dodging this way, then that, I hope
the wind stays lost in history.
That damn owl. For years I've waited for it
to speak up, announce the dream is a fraud,
send this insomniac back to bed
that haunts me more than the bats.

III

A weary stone drags its way toward the river.
Wanting to say I understand, ask
if it needs a hand, but just when I speak,
the owl swoops down, drowning my voice.

IV

If a god is around, he, she, or it must
wonder what link snapped when death
suddenly gasped, choked, then kept on chanting.
Now the only fugitives that see hope
alone are magnolias, happy
as the sea carries the storm off to sleep.
Their roots burrow like moles to the cliff.

V

Parading along the crevice of my eye,
forever doing its eight-legged tricks,
crow starts the long trek through the key-hole,
the air vents, the windows, off to the hills.
Exhausted, everyone watches for time
to shake our teeth until we skeleton.
Even the mountains hail the avalanche of sand
and shore, bursting from the sun's rip.

FOR THE PEOPLE WHO CAME
FROM THE MOON ⊁

They stalked deer for generations
down the mountain to the meadows
where the wind settles in our city's
mushroom heart. We called them
old friends and traded salmon
for their trophies. They were
the Snoqualmie and the river willow
echo their chants to children chasing
quail into the afternoon.

As carriers of the dream wheel
we sing of rain and thunder to the strangers
from our longhouses rising from the sea.
And when the evening logs burn down to masks
the hunters from the sky

will sleep as our guests in a light
that mutes both snowpeak and fern.
Circling the lake for the dawn
we enter the dream's spruce canyons
and see blue mallards land on the bow
of a lost canoe.

Our grandfathers with family buried
under clouds drifting from here to the waterfall,
by morning will put their ears against
the rotting cedar to hear the hoofbeats
of deer and elk pound tributes in our veins
the pulse of a new fire-winged season.

A BASKET OF THREE AVOCADOS ❧
for Natalie

The gift you offered me,
when I came home from the hospital,
is almost summer ripe,
this green and sun-spattered October day.
The skin, radiating warmth in my hands
and the color of your eyes,
stops the drone of yesterday's leafless sky
that faded the madronas, wrinkled
the kite the wind tore to wind-sticks.
This fruit gives birth to our words;
evades definition and history:
an abstract lyric unnecessary to learn;
a departure from melody and self.

AT A FRIEND'S HOUSEBOAT

for Charlotte

July light drops like drops
of moon into the water
and the water takes it deep.
We party with those who are
not afraid to cross
the shadows or the senses.
Imagination guides them through
the naked maze, the door
opening to the night.

The wars we never win pass
from our sight with the planets.
We don't wave knowing
they keep the circle.
By the wharf, madronas lift
us to the stars growing
sapphire, then silver in the lake.
Wild ducks take the wind
current to another sky.
On the porch, facing the Olympics,
our conversation reaches the sea;
picks huckleberries near La Push;
rocks time like a boat.
Inside the house, jazz rhythms
fling blue-note confetti.
And there, by the door,
a sculptured Orpheus on the floor
raises his hand to outreach the dark.
As if part of a larger composition,

Leo Kenney's "Numbers Coming Into Being,"
on the far wall, begin to move
down the side toward the water.
It would be a clock

that likes to swim. Adding
our own laughter and puns, we step
outside; the ocher air
flows under our arms; the long,
the short, the undulating waves.
While we dance on the edge
like moths, the evening returns
to its blue relief.

HOMAGE TO MARC CHAGALL (1887-1985) 🐝

Before his brush touches canvas,
the seven candles take turns
leaping through the window; flames
arc like a rainbow over Vitebsk farms
clear to the valleys on the moon.

In the far corner, a tattered juggler
tosses apples into the air
that fall back into his hands
like falling stars; then as a second
stroke makes its search across

to the other corner in the room,
the juggler decides to tumble
inside the blue cow's crystal ball,
seven more strokes, counting day and night
and pastures. He is joyous and no one

thinks this strange; besides, the town
stops raging for the winter solstice,
tries burying its lies in the goat's
footprints, fears under graveyard snowbells.
Quite happy for a moment, the synagogue

crier trades songs for hope of spring change.
Children, half asleep in mittens and hair coats,
meet on the path the bearded violinist
on their walk to the village school.
They watch their favorite alibi

strand notes on the poplar trees,
the blue spruce, the scarecrow's top hat;
laughing, the green rabbi puns the Czar
in Hebrew, and the snow-spotted crow, in Crow.
For decades, in the theater of the real,

police have rolled off the ghetto wall
like dice, tyrants like bowling pins.
Even these children in the Russian
village of his birth have witnessed
his palette's dance for women and art.

And each model has the memory of his hand,
his satyr's prance from dawn to sunset.
Like Renoir, Degas, Matisse and Picasso,
he accents her figure in a choreography of nuance.
In celebration of passion without mirrors,
the painter catches the blossom on the wing
from the "Sun at Poros," to give us
when windows and doors open to yellow haystacks.
Sniffing the herbal air as red as creation,
Eros hails the magician of color and shade,

and we turn willingly into scattered
snowballs, light figures melting in miracle.

ELEGY FOR LOUISE BOGAN ❧

Now that you are darker
than the February sod,
stark and blue with snowflakes,
your breath the air of stone—

I'll close my eyes and ears
to holly and sparrow,
the landmarks of loss—your voice
drowned in night's stream.

AT THE HOHOKAM RUINS ❧

for Barbara

I The Past

The fear of the ancient
we try leaving behind in the city,
step into the morning horned toads
catch in other light. The earth
whirrs with insects from each direction.
Flies weave in and out of our vision.
A lizard darts along the powdered path,
shy guardian of dust devils.
Quiet as the miles of cactus,
we stop and rest as a magpie
is startled into rising from the ground
to vanish with the stream of tiny
suns tossed by dawn.

II Skoaquik, Place of Snakes

It is here we remember
the Pima story of singing
to the rattlesnakes a chant
for a little rain, a sprout of seed,
the designs that reach the onyx horizon.
Far in the distance,
a coyote is intent on following
the turquoise wind.
What has it heard from the sky?
The dove abandoning the sagebrush shadow?
Reaching the gold circle's point,

we drag our feet in the dust,
speak to the howling faces we become
on the shattered vessels, clay figurines.

III Bone Shakers

Companion to the shrub grouse,
gopher, and butterfly, we hold
in our hands the reticent,
moon-necklaced lizard when
the evening's first star calls us home.
Here where the saguaro wrens
keep the language, feeling minds
its own wild calm; ages
even the banded gecko night stirred,
the one carrying the legend
down our spines, creating
a hive of sensation.
It touches us like a medicine bowl.

The wind rattles broken pots;
vibrates the village grave.
Reluctant to admit we
are strangers, we close our eyes
before turning back; see
the hawk lift the snake
to its rainbow arc.

CONSULTING AN ELDER POET ON AN ANTI-WAR POEM 🪰
for Elizabeth Bishop

You said to me that day,
"There's nothing you can do,"
and spoke of Auden's line:
"Poetry makes nothing happen."
And though I honor you,
especially your poems,
the objects you dipped in light,
then, left in the rainbow,
let slip from our sight,
I admitted, diving out of self,
a sweet woman's white caress,
the hundreds of lives and places
in books, failed to counter confusion.

You did agree that it
was Socrates who said
to his Athenian friends
that governments are only
governments with many heads
and cannot think as one.
That history continues to show
how they swing from war
to peace and back again,
in one wide gallow-sweep
just as the pendulum
of the world's clocks
returned its towns to craters.

Now I must ask myself,
fifteen cobalt-blue years later,
if the dust of each new war
that settles in our bones,
and deadens a generation,
is no more than negatives
of the Kennedys, King, and Lennon,
has less weight than what
we felt the day the Apollo
spaceship landed on the moon,
and Auden's line is true,
then why did you to the end,
live with the dark,
sing into your ruin?

LOVE POEM ❧

The twilight of your face,
the unknown bird in your voice,
draws me again to your eyes' green vision,

your song about that longest
moment, a moon vulnerability,
a Natalie I saw alone,

at Carolyn's party years ago,
where you called me to your side,
and I held my heart, cupped in shadow,

as an offering to your smile,
our soft-spoken isolation.

SLOW DANCER THAT NO ONE HEARS BUT YOU 🦋

She, the green singer, creature of waves,
interpreter of the moon's stone calendar,
fragrant path-finder through the forest, asks
you to dance with the ambivalence of the wind.
When she steps close to you, the calligraphy
of maple leaves reveal your vanishing tribe:
your totem's abstract vagabonds.

Her song that paints the owl's face blank
on the black mask of the Klallam hillside
suggests she may be reaching for your heart,
naked and trembling in the moonlight,
a bold flame dancing in her embrace.
Are you not the lover she has chosen
for the night? Temporarily outside

the clutches of the young at their easels,
her stare marks a serene eye of enclosure.
How she arrives at the start of your dream
drives you on and on through the field,
running from shadow to shadow, toward
her hand that is never within reach,
but appealing, so you go on, knowing she

is what is real, as important as your breath.
Forever smiling, her lusty pupils radiate
your desire, and she starts to set you free,
walk her fingers down your soul's back.
Now falling to sleep will be easier—

she leaves blue words to hold the wind
and you give each syllable to the women
who crossed your river.

TO THOSE UNITED BY CANKPE OPI 🐜

Grass hides its children in the beetle's
earthen bowl. Its legends are simple:
by noon, the wind digs into the plains
like coyote. Nothing leaves these
black hills but the worms burrowing
songs into tomorrow.
Under twilight's wing, howling
for the red and yellow, we dance
to the center of the sun,
begin the search for the path
from the ground. Each step
burns a new color into our smallest vein.
By the hour the women have weeped
beyond the trail of tears, the long march,
the young and old have claimed their scars.
Still, despair brings our children,
running down the night, sweet pollen
from the graves of warrior dreamers.

SEPTEMBER LIGHT 🐾

I

A blue as abstract as the ninth
night into umber—crows
fly beyond the field, the river willow;
all slows to an attrition of dusk.
Drawing me to the open door,
flies walk up and down the screen.

On the porch I'm no longer sure
these guests sound their origin.
I offer them water, honey, a Bach cantata,
but nothing else. Later, on the couch,
I sense one void empty into the main current,
green and vocal as an algae allegory.
Ocher light wanders about the room;
for the surprise I choose to wander with it,
muffled, gnarled, and conquered.

II

A white as peacock in the painting
on the opposite wall pauses
in the sunlight, changes the colors
and direction of the visible, as if
the strangers in the next apartment
had bolted us from their lives, sealed off
the music in our room.

Stepping up to the window to look
beyond, I start to find my figure in the land.

It is the blackbird's shadow.
The wind carries the clouds, the blackbird,
the season, and myself to the Cascade Mountains.
There lies the quiet, the stationary,
the rhythmical, the sky's yellow meditation
upon the earth. With the wind I sing
for my ancestors and my love. We'll gladly
warm to sleep when the night lets go.

Digging Out the Roots

1977

SONG FROM THE TOTEM MAKER ❧

Why not view your family's past
from a less weathered shore?
You have a chance to forgive your wounds.
For you were the boy who often wished
he had burned his ancestors' longhouse
to the ground. Besides, you could never
blame the village shaker;
it was his stories that brought you comfort.

They showed how to see the owl
settle in the four directions, hear
the river run for salmon's way.
They cleared the path to where First People
circled until your feelings had wings,
to ease the morning's weight on your eyelids,
bury your pride in confusion's cave.

And I offered you when young a light
burden, seven days of rain, and another storm.
You saw the water dreamers run away with hope:
Thunderbird because he's entombed in clay,
teeth, and shell; Raven because it can't see
the sun touch the crocus beneath the ferns
without laughing so hard it thunders.

The water dreamers also ran away
because blue jay watched the people miss his
humor, his praise to the women who swam
the river; whale because it's now desert dust.

Beaver because his last dam demolished
the rainbow that held up the stars.
Since beaver didn't keep his nose to the current,

the winter floods took his dam to another country.
And you never appreciated the time wolf
roamed through your terror of the forest's
destruction. But he'll stop when you stop
running from the dead and the cave drummers.
So the next dawn wolf calls to you,
listen to his rattle that shakes you to shore,

as it was your ignorance that started the tremor
that led the sharks to your dying village,
the dwindling stream inching toward the breakers.

STREET KID 🐾

I stand at a window that reaches
the sagebrush field and beyond
to the concentric rings of twilight—
Martinez, California, north of San Francisco.
Reaching for the earth and its shield,
the silence of the sun burns
my thirteen years into the hill
while the white breath of insects
whirrs and crawls down the glass
between the bars. But it is the meadowlark
warbling at the end of the fence
that sets me apart from the other boys,
the cool toughs playing ping pong,
dice and cards before lock-up.
When this new home stops playing the fox
with my memory as well as my nickname,
Injun Joe, thrown to me like a knife
by the pale ones, the Blacks, the Chicanos
growing lean as the solitude, I step
from the window into their elliptical stares,
then quietly into the darkness,
the room where my soul builds
a nest against the wall.

THE VISITOR ❧

He came to Walla Walla to see what he guessed
were friends, regain his soul, face the storm,
follow deer to the river, quiet in the dawn,
step softly like wind through wheat, he said.
He wasn't desperate; merely confident it was
the only way to breathe again while asleep:
his songs were sculptured ghosts, wretched,
bloody with violent roots, nomadic fractures,

burnt-out water drums. He wanted change. A return
to fiction; a new direction where he might collapse,
recognize his shadow in tomorrow's sunlight.
Lately, he missed his older brother, courage.
So, like the scarecrow who offers fear the season,
he whirls down the road like bunch grass.

THE OWL IN THE REARVIEW MIRROR 🦋

It was a miracle he glimpsed an owl sway
sideways through his eye. He watched it roll
back from the hills, hills ebbing like glaciers;
swing across the sky like a pendulum.
Does it follow stars through wheat fields
because hunger calls, or moon is luminous?
Does it tell him, not to ram the oak?
As is, the bird seems content to shift his roots,
plant him like a sapling in snow. For it
pulls him into the back seat and out the window
by the power of its agile, silent wing.
He is the mouse paralyzed by its shadow dance.
So he goes further, lets it drive him home,
leave his soul soaring for the yellow sky.

THE DICE CHANGER 🐾

Raven steals your name for an autumn joke:
buries you along with it under
the thickest hemlock known to chipmunks.
Too bad you were awake for the event.
He accuses you of asking all
the wrong questions over and over.
You attempt revolt to prove his medicine
wheel is cracked and filling up its own pit.

He hollers your face is unmasked and madness
has found a home. All stink and rotten fur,
he says to you, claims you had a choice
and forgot what it was. Now he says
your pain must run for the river,
the river for the wind.
He chuckles and the dark chatters, turning
you around until your shadow is the earth's.

TIDE BLOSSOMS ❧

She and I alone step down the shore.
I hold her close because she's a daughter of the sea.
We watch boats cross the jetty's corridor.

The autumn storm strikes our bodies with its lore
as the voices of the wind we hear and seek.
She and I alone step down the shore.

The clouds that spark return the blue to force;
the rain drowns out the breakers ebbing reefs.
We watch boats cross the jetty's corridor.

Sun-buoyed, kelp and cod drift along the shoal;
the terns dip green, turn shadow and are free.
She and I alone step down the shore.

Like a forest arrow this shield leaves us transformed;
salt and moon and sun compose our dream.
We watch boats cross the jetty's corridor.

When amber waves carve oysters to the core
a sandpiper darts over its slanting ground of peace.
She and I alone step down the shore.
We watch boats cross the jetty's corridor.

GRANDFATHER'S STORY ❧
for Francis Patsy

A dive into the Elwha river challenges fear.
By sunset Crow will show how to swim like salmon boy.
Under moonlit ferns it'll tell of your father,
on a ship far from Hadlock Bay and red cedars.
Perhaps your Italian father saw you chase gulls
but my guess is he was a sailor as blind as morning star.

Today we'll sing a round for morning star,
and unlike our rivers I'll speak of your fear,
but with the right song, fears will change to gulls,
though I barely said to you, my daughter's boy,
that a winter storm can split you like a cedar;
you need never know the sea chose your father.

Instead, each season you'll learn of your father,
and so live to wonder at the morning star.
As Raven buries your pain under cedars
our Klallam dancers will chant of love netting fear,
summer greens that nourish your growth as a boy.
And World War II could've killed your father and the gulls.

Your story will end when dawn touches a nest of gulls
then sinks the ship so the sailor
can return to answer what you ask as a boy.
It might ease a father stoned by morning star.
I'll throw sand on the embers of your fear,
guide you riding the storms, nightmares rotting cedars.

Blue jay will join us talking with the cedars
as the wingless sailor drowns, no surprise to gulls.
You'll dig through the family ruins to ease the fear.
On shore you'll ask the wind to name your father
but it will be as deaf as the morning star.
As Trickster bears the tribe, the river bears its boy.

So your father's no more a mystery than this, my boy—
beneath this northwest sky and Klallam cedars,
your father's ship steams like the morning star,
and when you laugh the coast will arc with gulls,
the sweatlodge cleanse you of your father.
And when a crow leads us home we'll hear no fears.

So night will no longer possess you like a white fear
when I give the story back to the Hadlock cedars
as you zig-zag down the beach, your feet gulls' prints.

DIGGING OUT THE ROOTS ❧

Thirteen pieces of silver means bad luck,
if I think there are thirteen rolls
to live, and see only the gambler,
and not the road or the forest.

So I return as often as possible
to the ruins of my Klallam ancestors,
N'huia-wulsh, their white fir village,
count the rain seasons since
my grandfather fell to the ground like cedar,
where his flesh and bones settled
in the dense regions of fern and snail.
I am back to carve for the last time
the red moon out of my native sky.

This elder that took me canoeing on the Hoko
and Elwha rivers sang to the clouds
that he knew trouble is free and floating.
And once, when I was nine or ten,
this gentle story teller became furious,
struck me with a willow, for defying him,
ruining my clothes and shoes
by slipping into the water countless times
as I snapped up a rockfish by its gills,
then slapped its head against a rock.
The welts that appeared that blood-bright
day are the muscles that link
my arms to my back.

A fern-shy teen in the Navy, I threatened
most of my childhood fears with a life
surrounded by irate ravens. When I
was confined in a Marine Brig for drinking
as a minor, the brig warden called me
an idiot and a wetback, so I slashed
away at him in delirium until the ants
marched back into my blood, in those
days that shook me into manhood.

Home again, I met a rare woman and we married.
Beside a yellow tub I watched her dry
her thighs. Her smile lit my skin,
the walls with her dance, the play of our kiss
to the end of dawn, and sleep.

We shared the labyrinth of two autumns.
The scents of Seattle were then alive,
pine, rose, magnolia, azalea,
the sea a magic drummer,
before the storm blew our dream out the window,
leaving us two unknown statues.
The birth of a son our best poem.

Tossing a bottle of the past to the river,
I ducked when the bottle crashed through
the mirror and broke against my skull,
before a new woman opened my eyes and I sighed,
when she whispered not to move,
and her hands danced right down my back.

After painting the apartment in the same
light as the sun gives to a tahoma
meadow, we lived to discover its lakes
and trails. I would carry her from the living
room to our green bed, gently hold
her warm breasts and body to my chest.

Neither she nor I understood when or how
it all began to crumble in our hands.
Having learned to love with irony,
we were careful and as soft as the candle.
Hearing music chip pieces off the moon,
no one could tell us our flesh would not
wrinkle and crack like paper, our bones
not split any less than the logs
in the winter fire.

We hunted for a ring, from city to train,
window to valley, stream to mountain,
then saw the clouds pass and leave the wind
and us on a hill within tulip waves.

We were unable yet to bare the silence,
so the failure rolled down her cheeks
to become a tiny lake in my heart, the day
our shadows attacked us like rats,
chased us down the subway to the street.

On the nights the Trickster mocked my totems,
I pushed my fist into the nightmare's eye,
the fork-tongued clown who stole
my dream-wheel. But panic left me alone
when she handed my cottage key to the ghosts
of my wife and son. What memory burns
now is the confusion of naming.

Under this sun of laurel there seem
to be fewer errors to trust,
humility to tear, puzzles for this cedar
crow's descent; and by summer
the ocher wind will trade these
remaining feathers for the chance
to reach one more open field.

THE WAY ❧

The smog-edge sky blurs the lillies and his eye
like a cataract. The pond is abstract, a green
ripple flowing through the frog and dragon-fly.
The wind tells him nothing about direction:
it refuses to give one name to summer.
He won't laugh at the frog, if it won't laugh.
He's kept moving to purge the loneliness.
At thirty-three, it's neither self-indulgence
nor a loser's plea to wear a freedom mask.
He's maskless as the birch and half as white,
and the rust collecting sun leaves him bone-naked:
although a cedar child from birth, earth pitched,
today, he's opaque, snared. So he wonders if he
swam the Hoko river as a boy to reach his shade.

SONG OF THE ROAD

I stayed on the wrong road to play the breaks,
see if the street would change the nerves' form.
Even as a boy joy sometimes tagged me.
So today I rattle with exhilaration.
And stopped the search for my father's grave.
I need no more purge his indifference
than a wolf needs the company of the dead.
During my body's best years it was grief
sapped my strength because of my mother's many-
bladed bitchiness when I was young.
The truth seems it was my father's absence,
and what's necessary is to act the man he wasn't.
From this mound to run as white as the wind,
watch for the laurel woman who offers her hand.
Oh then, oh then, I could laugh at the buzzard
when it feeds on my remaining ocher grains!

THANKING SOME ELDER POETS ✍

When feelings of self-pity crawl
down my back like a rose-spider,
I remember your parodies of the sentimentalist,
feel ashamed. For only when I live
the failure is my shadow mine
and I once more a man of seed.

RUNNER FOR THE THUNDER, CLOUD AND RAIN ☙

I am the fox on the roam
for your changes, the salmon who leaps
through sunlight on the river,
the mushroom sprouting in the rain,
the bear who dances round
and round the gentle woman,
the guardian of our infant children,
the carrier of the Elders' flame.
I sing for the dead,
the lovers and their rainbow!

THE WHEEL OF RETURN 🏵

I dig up and quickly bury the old mistakes,
to stay alive behind my snow shield.
A fugitive from suicide in Baltimore,
I hunt for the legends in the sky
whirling from my head the puzzle
of my one epileptic seizure.
Yet I am determined to reach the labyrinth
of the open window, where you blossom
like an orange chrysanthemum.
Every turn of this cycle rises or rests
in the field of your echo.

THE HERMIT 🦋
after Kozinski's novel The Painted Bird

Without family, Lekh appeared one morning
in the village, hunched over his past
like an abandoned crane. He was
through with wandering from nest to tree,
forest to village. He was the collector
of birds. But when he reached the alders,
the Middle Ages, he was turned around
by the passion of Ludmila. So each step
drove desire a little deeper into his flesh,
brought him closer to her mirage,
where his scars would bloom with the marigolds.

The villagers called him half bird, half tree,
soulless, placed bets on whether the devil
sent him to mock their already haunted lives.
Hidden behind the moss and fern,
the children stared at the man of knotted pine
and claw, yet hummed in silence his songs
about the snow fools in his life.

Rumor spread like a spider's web
over Lekh's retreat. Then slowly as if
enraged by the stars, Ludmila's indifference,
he began to paint his bird's multi-colors,
rainbow hues, set them free to die.

After tossing the last dove into the blood
hot sky, he was last seen running
from his hut for the river, to rip

the clothes from his body that named
him Lekh, spit at the ghosts devouring
his mind like ants.

TESS ONE WINTER IN THE FIELD 🎕

She glances round to see snow settle on the hill,
feels a flake melt against her palm, coarsen her mood.
She shudders at the fickle vacancies of the blizzard,
its drifts that cannot fill the emptiness of pails.

Ice tufts cup the hedgerow's thorns;
grow so heavy they crumble from within.
The terrain flows crystal in her blood.
The men are brooding, something must be wrong.

Cobwebs hang here and there along stonewalls;
reveal lines where they are usually concealed.
A haze leaves the land birch white; falls
like loops of silk on barn and plough.

Because the snow now curdles into slush,
a scarecrow tips his hat to sheep and cow.
Suddenly, birds circle from the frozen North;
shabby birds whose eyes are bright and black.

She wonders, do these creatures carry a nightmare
the farm of Flintcomb-Ash will soon imagine?
When the sky is struck by these brazen birds,
she and another maid under their amorphous wings

dismiss the feathered anomalies with a shrug.
They want only to abandon the digging and the cold,
sing again the harvest songs of youth,
block the wind burying the cow's bell in the mud.

Songs For the Harvester of Dreams

1981

DREAM OF THE BURNING LONGHOUSE 🦌

Spinning away from the center,
lost to the flames, the old ones
break down to shadow and ash.
Without their songs of growing
brittle as the hemlocks,
will I be banished from my blood's country?
Has my heart thrown the drum to the earth?
My spirit forgotten its song to the mountains?
Oh my body, are you telling our story to the cave?

KLALLAM SONG

O woman who sleeps in my heart,
I have come to light
the deep pools of your eyes,
dance into the circle of your dream.
Because I am poor, a maker of song,
I fly slowly round the luminous
branches to be a figure
of your moontree, offer you the fire,
O woman who sleeps in my heart.

WOMAN OF THE MOON

Grandmother says
she can't be seen with the eye,
but the dream.
Dances in your shadow when you
offer her beads shaped by the seasons.
She will find the colors of your heart
if she desires to balance
your vision by her own,
your nerves with her embrace,
her body naked in your arms.

RAVEN DANCER 🦎

He rises from the hemlock side of the moon—
starts the fire for the people,
to warm the lost, the weary, the homeless.
When his eyes find you, the old ones
will shape the ashes, your soul clapping
in the light of anonymity.

WOLVES ❧

Once shy nomads from Pacific slopes
to fireweed meadows and tide flats,
they would call us from our longhouses
with their white-throated song.
When the wind returned the seven breaths
the snowfall yelped from dawn to dusk.
The hunters in our family always waited
like shadows to hear our brothers'
winter count take us back to the deer,
the running beauty striking off their hooves.

THE WORDS 🦎

They tell us to forget about them,
don't be sad when they return to the sea
with their legends and our dreams;
the loss is joyous, the way the winter
finds its home in our blood.
They tell us to move on like the water,
the earth embracing its many leaves.
So when we can't name who locked
us inside darkness's inner cave,
loosened the dirt under our feet
with the old fears of defeat, death, love,
they will come prancing round our village
once more with the loon's shrill inscape,
carve a path out of the cave clear
to the sea's mouth, the crab's spiny trail.
They tell us to swim for the dawn,
kiss the stars goodbye as if two fish
leaping between the sun and moon.

THE CANOE

Fungus buried, mossy as Elwha river mist,
it is the remains of Old Man's totem.
On this earth you must breathe like the evergreens
where this elder carved lean animals
of the sun on his paddles, or Seatco
will beat you songless,
blind you to what these shadows yield.

HERON AT LOW TIDE ❧

No wonder Young Patsy,
my great-grandfather,
saw this bird as the sun's
first born. It stands

in a tide-flat pool
at seven in the morning
with only its head and legs
visible in the fog stream,
salty and as steady as a reed.

So when it jumps upward
in a great blue break
to drift sideways down Oak Bay
I can almost feel it snap
once for Young Patsy.

BALD EAGLE 🪶

In a long cloud-patch fall toward the river,
his wingtip gathers the force of sun,
wind and rain from sea to valley.
His dive cascades down your spine.
It spirals through your mind watching
its talons curve into the wave
rising and dropping like salmon.

Seasons later you swear to friends
this grandfather, perched on the black ledge,
underneath your retina that fed
the fear with the greatest hunger,
showed you its precarious shift
from the sky's rolling-over prism
to the shaggy tilt of the morning star.

As the earth slides away from the river
to a dream, this white-headed drifter
of green air rushes back up your spine
with the story of how you must live
and die with the animals you destroy.
Otherwise, how can his shriek greet your bones?

SPIDER ⚹

Stop, friends, spin with me past
the morning rain, the morning rain.
Touch the yellow, orange, and green threads—
feel the thunder that passed my house!

And if by chance, by accidental dance,
we meet where the meadow's a violet ledge,
don't be frightened by my traces,
they were woven to delight the sun.

> There are things about us
> too beautiful to lose;
> our many-colored song
> not even the Raven knows.

THE ART OF CLAY 🌿

The years in the blood keep us naked to the bone.
So many hours of darkness we fail to sublimate.
Light breaks down the days to printless stone.

I sing what I sang before, it's the dream alone.
We fall like the sun when the moon's our fate.
The years in the blood keep us naked to the bone.

I wouldn't reach your hand, if I feared the dark alone;
my heart's a river, but is not chilled with hate.
Light breaks down the days to printless stone.

We dance for memory because it's here on loan.
And as the music stops, nothing's lost but the date.
The years in the blood keep us naked to the bone.

How round the sky, how the planets drink the unknown.
I gently touch; your eyes show it isn't late.
Light breaks down the days to printless stone.

What figures in this clay; gives a sharper hone?
What turns the spirit white? Wanting to abbreviate?
The years in the blood keep us naked to the bone.
Light breaks down the days to printless stone.

DRAWINGS OF THE SONG ANIMALS 🦎

I

Treefrog winks without springing
from its elderberry hideaway.
Before the day is buried in dusk
I will trust the crumbling earth.

II

Foghorns, the bleached absence
of the Cascade and Olympic mountains.
The bay sleeps in a shell of haze.
Anchorless as the night,
the blue-winged teal dredges for the moon.

III

Thistle plumed,
a raccoon pillages my garbage.
When did we plug its nose with concrete?
Whose eyes lie embedded in chemicals?

IV

Dams abridge the Columbia Basin.
On the rim of a rotting barrel,
a crow. The impossible remains
of a cedar man's salmon trap.

V

Deer crossing the freeway—
don't graze near us, don't trust our signs.
We hold your ears in our teeth,
your hoofs on our dashboards.

VI

Shells, gravel musings from the deep,
dwellings from the labyrinth of worms.
Crabs crawl sideways into another layer of dark.

VII

Bumblebee,
a husk of winter and the wind.
I will dance in your field
if the void is in bloom.

VIII

A lizard appears, startled by my basket
of blackberries. In the white
of the afternoon we are lost to the stream.
Forty years to unmask the soul!

THE MUSICIAN 🦎

Your notes built
a place of refuge
in our house. You
often played on sheets
of dawn. But your
visits were brief
retrievals lost
by dusk, our coming
of age, time's eraser.

We miss you most
when the snow falls
and hardens to crystal,
where the attic mice
used to sleep
in the candlelight
we burnt on the stairs
to your guest-room.
Now they're gone too.

You're the secret sharer.
What moon went bronze,
what measures kept
the color of the peonies
at the sonata's end?
Your sound, a sapphire
fountain, transparent
as the August river.
The night rhythms

these last few years
roll flat in your absence.
Oh why did you quit
our piano and the city
unannounced? What
distant melody took
you from our white pines?
We feel marginal.
Yet our lined-faces

keep returning to
the hours you composed
the verbena sky vibrato.
In our imperfections
and the pizzicato
refrains of autumn's
first adventurous leaves,
we ask the wind
to open the window,
play the piano, let
our souls be the poplars
echoing and repopulating
your concerto of the lake.

ALBUM OF THE LABYRINTH ❧

I

She left me a room with a few
pieces of her sculpture.
Since two seasons turned gray,
I feel this wound is her gift.

II

When a downcast face rose with a smile,
greeted me among the market strangers,
my feet of clay loosened
from the weight of my being.

III

The woman who climbed the iron stairs
to the tower of last night's dream.
Was she coming or going?
And was it me standing at the window
waiting for her to change the room?
What we separate or what separates us?

IV

I learn to keep the dream wheel nearby.
Its soul is more than likely mine.
If it dies my spirit will be yours.

V

Do we knock down the doors with our
lives to meet the storm's center?
Could this be our song of despair?

VI

The animals that circle the nightmare
do not lead me to fear, but myself.
What they never roar I hear the nights
when I am a verb of solitude.

VII

As my feet touched the street
I knew I should have spoken to the woman
on the bus who offered me her isolation.
Was cruelty the failure
of my voice to answer chance?

VIII

I go on writing these words
because they go on taking me beyond themselves.
The truth lies between connections.

IX

Mostly we chose to fidget at the wall.
What we lost was the nerve, not the wall.

X

We counted too much on pain;
learned after it shuffled on and abandoned
us to our scars that it
was visiting in the body of joy.
Yet we can't refrain from calling
silence the fugitive.

XI

Out of pity I stand before the mirror;
I have a question for it;
just as I am about to release the demons
the mirror crumbles. Still,
years later I think it answered.

XII

When you begin hiding the cards
you have already lost the game.

XIII

I was glad to be born on Friday,
the thirteenth, in icy winds.
From this hoop I inherited
my histories of ruin.

XIV

I bury in memory's shifting mud
the promises I seldom keep.
Otherwise, why the need for failure?

XV

Autumn calls me the dream's myopic student.
I call it the Trickster;
when the next summer ends
I will grow closer to the small.

XVI

If I could choose one road in my life
Death could keep its song.

XVII

There are friends who call me a hermit.
The last woman who entered
and exited my house agreed with them.
Why didn't they see the crow
outside their window was my heart
turning to cedar in their names?

XVIII

As a tribute to the apparitions
I become, I zig-zag my way
from city to city, country to country;
sing to the void, to what humbles me.

III

FIRST SPRING ❧

Drifting off the wheel of a past
looking like a redskin American gothic,
staring through forty-one years
of rain-pelted windows, I bear
with modest grace, diminished nerves,
narrowing light, half-formed figures:
the memories floating in purgatory.

Renting a small house, the first
in fifteen years, I admire each hour
the diffidence of the elders walking by,
their snow-cave eyes, their hands
dancing like puppets. When a lost love
calls, having abandoned another,
I say,—*sorry, sorry, I'm too*

busy with the friends still left.
I'll call you. The lie of copper on my tongue.
Why tell her they're the birds at the feeder,
bees in the lilacs, roses, and plum trees,
books on the shelves and everywhere,
paintings on the walls, wind at the door
and on the roof?

> It is called giving your body
> a river to jump in to,
> it is called giving your brain cells
> a field to get planted in.
> It is called standing on your head

before the women you lost,
sleeping in the embers of your name.

New Poems

1978

APOLOGY 🜚

But a man cannot learn heroism from another,
he owes the world some death of his own invention.
          "Dying Away" / William Meredith

Great Uncle Joe,
can you hear me keen?
My temples now as salt and pepper as yours,
I am a weed in the wind by the side of your house.

I still awaken in the night
to the moment you said, *don't,*
when my eyes rolled and snagged.
You knew I had no choice but to follow
my mind pulling me so close to the elder
in the next bed that my breath was his,
and his mine. Trapped in the tide
of confusion I fought for the courage
that would keep my knees from knocking
against your bed, my head from spinning
out the door. You then told of how
your own youth snapped nerve by nerve.

Later, you admitted that your neighbor
had died that morning. No, you
did not shake your head in loathing.
Instead, you spoke in the way of your ancestors,

the Klallams, Swinomish, and Snohomish,
that it was good I had turned from him
whose owl had torn a hole in the window.

Great Uncle Joe,
can you hear me keen?
I am a weed in the light of your totem,
the hawk, because your face was free of scorn;

a weed uprooted with shame
over two decades after your death,
yet loyal to your path, my grandfather's,
and your sister's who gave me
your father's name, why, I don't know.
Cedar man, I bury my youth on your land;
its red earth shields my song
woven into the years for you

and the body of rock on Old Patsy's mound,
for mine, chanting to be near yours,
when I am the elder in the next bed.

THE REALITY OF AUTUMN 🎋

In my season as red as the red-breasted
woodpecker, I am the parts I fall from;
the urban accidents climbing from the ditch,
the years in reverse before eclipse;
the voices cracking like pods,
too weary to break the glass wheels
of the mirror, dance with the cubistic
caravan, the teeter-totter benefactors.

As the incurables in the photographs fade
with the sun, the day withdraws, takes
the fire, what I built from scars,
the earth, the mythology of dream.
What does it matter that I am
the animal whose one pliant structure
dies a song? So I look for the birth
of myself once more in the eyes of a woman
whose seesaw gift is joy and pain.
To mold the dark to the dark.

WINTER IN NEW YORK ❧

It is the swish and swirl of rain and snow,
the brief encounter with the sun,
the storm's signature that changes him.
Over the sidewalk there are leaves
chasing leaves in wider and wider circles,
in smaller and smaller number,

until at the center, the wind lies
so still on the ground, he wonders
if it is going to sound again,
whirl back from the drain,
but the symphony of aspen promises
with its bridge between skyscrapers,

lightly scores the sky-hued voices
with an ascending rondo of spring,
a faint ballet of sleet and sunshine.
Stepping nearly home, he looks down
the street for someone to share
the joy of his burden, its twists

and turns, low and high trills.
Without a person in sight, he decides
to dance with the creature veering
through dusk, the enveloping dark.
Now in rhythm with the conductor
he joins the gusty artist drawing notes

on gate, puddle, lamp post, and circles
his shadow keeping time, then enters
the brownstone, cold and wet,
but clean of fear and trembling.

SPRING CURRENTS ❦
for Robin

We slip into night's deeper layers,
to untangle ourselves from the city's smog,
escape it for the day.
At the start of the mountain path
we hear the aspen's trail,
the slow, then swift wind gusts,
March figures along the Elwha banks,
theme of last nights' conversation;
the way this river rolls off its banks
into the earth, taking us back to when
you almost drowned as a child
in a stream by your house.

By the river my ancestors called
the child who swims into dawn,
I point to a path angling up the mountain
to pine, avalanche lily, and eagle.
I tell you of an old promise to my grandfather,
to follow that path to the top
for a dive into glacial pools to thank
the water spirits, since it was his chant
that drew us here. The rapids
say goodbye at the willow opening.
As the sun approaches the meadow
the afternoon light is yellow cinquefoil.

High above the crows, snowpeaks keep the stars;
from each crest the colors of the slopes
melt seaward to join the seeds'

airy palpitations settling in the valley,
the wind-spored sky.
Around the bend the sea is a stroke
of moss and rockbed.
I dip my hands into the flow.
The right's a minnow
honing for the taste of the current,
the left, a black bear
pawing dusk in a dream of blue huckleberries.
Together our one and only time
we drift like treefrogs in the mist
on the madrona tree hanging over the river.

SUMMER TRANSPARENCIES

I

Although her touch held the fragments
in place, a microbe explosion
claims his heart. He has stared unblinkingly
at the wall of her absence.

II

They spent the nights battling demons,
the days battling themselves.
Even before it was too late
they quit asking what animal is
native to the maze.

III

A piece of glass half buried in sand.
Light roots mine the obsolete.
Yet the man in his shadow
sings for this home among rocks.

IV

The painter and the poet traded stories,
several circles of themselves last night.
When leaving her apartment he noticed
that in the morning even the cats treking
oblivion find a corner in the dark.

V

The clouds carve no exits in the sky,
so the mountains turn to the sea,
the insects, earth. For patience
and the keen ear that's deaf,
he holds a cup of rain in his hands.

VI

A map of rivers. The fish under water
weave their lives into the net;
he swims with them as the dream passes.

VII

He tried making his home on Puget Sound
a chamber for her song.
The storm says he would know cruelty
if he had never known her.

VIII

The mist, the cold, how does he embrace
the loss as his own?

IX

The wind in the weathervane.
The flow north through pine.
He stops for fallen cones:
the hard edges of summer.

THE WATERFALL SONG ❧
for Rona

From their first dawn, he embraced the night sensations;
she who danced with him into the burning words.
He wanted to feel her turn as the river turns,
she who danced with him into the burning words.

He stepped toward the song she offered in the dark;
she whose voice could stir the sparrow's heart.
He asked for her hand because his life was there.
She whose voice could stir the sparrow's heart.

He landscaped her home with the rarest stone;
she planted the seeds that brought the wild to bloom.
He carved her a bird the water filled with spirit.
She planted the seeds that brought the wild to bloom.

He saw from her eyes the waterfall was blue;
and it was she that changed the seasons of the wind.
And in their solitude he gave nakedness the field,
since it was she who kept the colors in the fall.

MEDITATION ON VISITING
HURRICANE RIDGE ❧

The climb up the trail to the ridge
will be slow and steady,
the view passionless and acute.
The sky point, setting the direction,
from off the memory for breaking ground,
will cross our path like an osprey's eye,
far above the cloud banks,
floating within sky-currents,
the dance of hanging between night and day,
where cedar and star settle with the ants
and mosquitos on the horizon.

The climb will be slow and steady,
an impregnating flow of sunlight
to follow back down the mountains, while
the nerves, the elders of the blood,
trace their roots to the edge,
to lichen, rock, and crow,
coming to rest with the molecular,
the lava layers exposed to eternity.

When the vein pulse in our toes is the sky's,
we will hear the earth's core shift.

With the sky pounding in our veins,
the snow under our feet will
shape for our children the rivers
of these mountains, these dead pines,
the windbreakers, bleached white as the sun.

Even the deer family we watched
near the forest and valley below
will one day leave footprints to chance
on the snow for others climbing
beyond themselves for the lost connection.

With the sky pounding in our veins,
we touch the earth to unknot the spine.

THE PASSENGER ❦

He finds a room without exits,
his breaths the air of accident.

The bait he left at each corner
a week ago is still there.
The rats have heard him call;
seen him refused room-service.
They have watched him solitaire,
shuffle the cards day and night,
but they run their own hazards;
aliases; bright spots in the trap.

His oblong limbs untwisting from
the dream catch no morning sun.

He, like the totaled car outside,
is out of running parts;
bruised muscles stripped by night.
The gun on the bedside table
suggests he deal in the losses, the ace
that'll lance survival at the bone.

FOUR MOBILES AFTER AN
ALEXANDER CALDER RETROSPECTIVE ❧

for Marc, my son

I

Four blue rings, a family of stars;
the old sky roamers bounce down
the cobble-stones of our dreams—
swirl between your dash and my dot.

II

Through a hole in the white ring
a flight of geese uncoils like the dawn
the earth went flat;
they arc back into the ring
when a young woman puts a feather in her hair,
a young man, a bell on his toe.

III

Circling our heads on a green-glowing wire,
a clown, leading the elephants on parade
in the ring below, blows his horn
for the poodle balancing a yellow ball on its nose,
then hails the children who skip in from the rain.

IV

An orange ring repeats the motions of the trapeze
artist hanging from the ceiling by her teeth.
When she stops we spin and spin and spin
like the scattered petals of New York
asters in Central Park.

THE TRAVELER 🦋

He still believes by middle-age
that freedom is a bread
to break every day. He wants
to go on resisting the narrow,
search for what form of rose will grow
from a plane, a train,
a candlelit cafe.

He thinks to be another stranger
in the night is perfect;
night figures are seldom wasted.
He welcomes the accidental,
the unknown woman he might meet.
To the hour, he stumbles
with the blind for sight.

He walks in the country when the sky
clears. In the town
of Kinderdijk, windmills
hint of the tenth century.
Far from his red earth,
he mourns what the Dutch have lost,
seeing the world is out
of balance even there.

The days spent in museums make
him weary but the Brueghels,
Goyas, Rubens mark their worth.
From Amsterdam to Paris

to Copenhagen, his spirit seeks to mix
his life like the colors on their palettes,
while his body sips its sherry.
To enjoy the people, the speech,
the cadence of train and bus
and boat, he empties his mind
of the global pollution,
the bottles and cans and stench
of each consumer institution,
all obsessions, why
his family calls him odd.

His woman friend says the storms
could be worse, he should
explore the windfunneled sand hills,
the force, face the sea,
let mind and body divorce and remarry,
navigate the winter course.

Though fond of her and the Netherlands,
he mentions the inverted scenes,
the salmon self that smells
nuclear rain, nuclear thunder, our blue
labyrinth of pain, the iceburg
he slept on through recent dreams.

Who hasn't thought these clouds might
ignite the globe, their
ominous showers penetrate our flesh,

soak us in their radial,
atmospheric mesh?
Who hasn't heard his own blood
dry at the bone?

But perhaps one morning he'll awake
to find it has been
merely an outhouse joke of Raven.
Now a stone mask, there is the chance
his will is getting even,
found the path to being a sand grain.

THE TARGET ❧

You drop the book to the floor
as the door-bell rings its echo of time:
it's your life's clan, feathered in guilt and sweat.
You sit out another sober night,
surrounded by the paintings and bookcases
crowding you from your bachelor's apartment,
while saving you from the recent history,
the failed romance, long unemployment,
middle-age blackouts, the deaths of relatives
and friends, the con man's trivia,
the freakshow mockeries that embalm us.

You accepted long ago art's impotence
in the face of politics; nevertheless,
it is the arts that give you wings
to escape your own worm pits,
the failures building pyramids to the ceiling.
So you read after twenty years,
Camus's *The Myth of Sisyphus,*
Shakespeare's *Hamlet* and *King Lear*

to appease the unwelcome trickster,
you, when a kid with no place to run:
the self you thought had hung itself
from the rafters of a garage, now as blurred
a memory as the girl who sheltered you.
Casually dancing in off the avenue,
whistling your blues and blacks and grays,
he shakes the dice in his closed fist,

rolls them to the carpet's edge,
then kicks the loaded .45 to your feet.
Always the clown, he winks and says:
"Guess who has come to a target?"

MAGGIE ❧

She skips on to the day's next blue radius,
a tulip weaving down the summer hill.

She circles with the sun on a wind beat,
her dress, the color of its equinox.

She inhales the impossible, light's fragrances.
When she blows a kiss to the Monarch,

death loses the laughter, the wheel rolling
back, the air. Just nine, cruelty hasn't

flipped her spine like a penny, chance
mined her dream with its arbitrary surprise.

Even the lilacs in her hair haven't heard
the earth call with its tuning fork of bees.

And when she swirls round her home on a dare,
even the rain begins to fall yellow.

IN THE AGE WHEN SOMEONE IS ALWAYS LEAVING ๕

I

You need to hear the red pulse-beat of the flower,
the quince's dirt-deep side, as if you're the air;
you need to quit counting on tomorrow, the hour,
step backwards all the way down the stair.

You could give yourself and her absence to spring,
imagine how the next move might cancel rage,
or, better still, beat itself into a new wing.
There are ways to renew your heritage.

Regard: the street door opens another door,
where the wind's the voice of no reply.
Branch in to black like the maple with sundown.
Put your back to the wall you won't deny.

If you dream, let it strike from nature's sphere,
keep the puzzle in your head like stars the year.

II

Since months pass, you seek an untried course,
paint a hole through the ceiling and split the cell.
Now the earth's a petal sea, April's light force,
you see it was more than sex, her green sighs, you felt.

The ground is gain, traces no contours of her face,
nor is her body near to punctuate the pain—
the sky's Picasso blue, clouds separate and fade,
lilac and bee accent the air, drowsy and sane.

In pulling garden weeds, you absorb the thought,
since she is out of reach, wrestle dread.
Yet at a time when every clod breaks hard,
you work inside your skin and swear you'll mend.

Stone fed, as native as the pine, you make peace,
conclude, she was your Claire de Lune, and real.

LINES FOR ROETHKE TWENTY YEARS AFTER HIS DEATH ❧

I

You asked us to hear the softest vocable of wind,
whether slow or swift, rising or falling to earth;
its fragments will drop in to place in the end.
You said, believe, endure, the ironies of birth!
If we succeeded in sleeping like thorns on a rose,
the nerves awake to the pulse, folklore of the sun,
the interior drifts may loosen, the nights freeze,
the passions whirl, not ramble until undone.
And no one colors the years black, but crow,
retouches the ruins, fakes the moon, pocks the beach.
Laugh right back, you sang, let it take hold,
it'll grow bored, forget whoever may be in reach.
Let your hand trace the riddle on the wave,
rejoice in the tale that leaves the ear a cave.

II

To give each death its light reflects the maze,
the promise bacteria also favor green.
You secretly burned your tracks to fan the blaze,
and warned the world'll tell us what to dream.
This is why you spoke in tongues to the vine,
wren, snail, bear, sloth, and swamp air.
You almost found an island without decline,
where roots kept your soul exposed to every layer.
You suggested we see the spirit's gift in the eye,
but the eye in the gut, the slug in the mossy field.
Taught us ghosts can love as well as mortify,
yet the heart's the actor; we must bow and yield.
When your body's a wheat impulse, nothing's stale;
even thunder's crack is music to the whale.

III

The mind follows currents deeper than any fish,
gropes with otter and duck for food in the river,
it knows water tumbling over rocks restores the flesh,
awaits the moon in the poplars, its first cover—
to meet extremes face to face, seed to seed,
be anonymous as a fly's grave at dark.
Fill solitude with creatures other than your need;
let the wolf take your shade, teach you to bark.
How to breathe with form? Proceed like the worm;
help desire cross the bridge of the brain;
it relieves paralysis, the wrong turn.
Kiss the petals before and after rain.
Climb out of yourself; edge in close to fate;
smell mortality like the lily on the lake.

IV

You scolded, we can't spin the wheel that spins night,
can't shed the scars from birth like old skin.
Better drift in your bones than with the kite;
better croak with blue jay, picking at the limb.
And imagination swims for the Muse on her shell,
while her tribe tickles our inner ear.
Don't mistake; her cymbals taunt the devil;
as she dances, he shreds like pulp all year.
So we can dream, barter seasons with the dead,
if we accept that, when they embrace, they cling.
All's headless as love, you sighed, all shapes you wed,
your senses burnt-orange, bold stranger to nothing
but yourself, your lips as white as Michigan snow.
Show us again how to reap the fire and glow.

FRIENDSHIP IN KLALLAM COUNTRY ❧

Grandfather told me when I was a boy
that Lucy Patsy, my great-grandmother,
wife of Young Patsy, son of the elder
of Hadlock Bay village, spoke
for generations of our Klallam tradition.
She said the family greeted a stranger
into the village circle like the wind,
since even a stranger would know
most of our days are littered
with the many-forked cackle of the raven,
blue jay, and the bones of memory.
She sang that the fires stayed lit to morning
when you welcomed the guest to our long-house,
family of smoked salmon and oyster—

it is because of the stranger we exist,
can tell him the story of our children
digging clams on our seal-whiskered shore.
Let him step like sunlight through the door,
enter and seat himself by the fire.
It is as green as the sea rose and moss.
The steps through our house echo
the voices of the rivers, the Elwha and Hoko,
rolling down the mountains we call ancestors.
So offer him our Salish totems like a robe;
root our guest in the red cedar earth
near the path, pulsing like the tide.

AT THE INTERNATIONAL
POETRY FESTIVAL 🦂

I awoke to the flight of a tern skimming the canal,
to cars swerving round a packed and portly trolley.
Thriving, the city rides the morning rail.
Street voices dangle in the present, coffeed and busy.
Rotterdam's all commerce, bustling and concentric—
gulls and peddlars give birth and die on water,
pass under, over bridges, while the traffic
honks its way to market, fades to a ship's blur.
The light's a balcony, Vermeer's or Van Gogh's—
June palette of window-boxes: geraniums and pansies.
I almost touch the Rembrandt-sky, grey-orange,
the corner-stalls, the red and yellow poppies.
In Holland, my pain's a skull, void of face;
like the cypress, I leave shadows to their surface.

ROUND DANCE 🦎

Sweet woman, come dance with me,
let's touch earth's center, so no one's a stranger,
I welcome you on this Klallam path
as the flicker does whose tapping beak
is as moon-inlaid as the cedar bark.
O step with me round the fire,
enter the circle the blood sparks,
      the heart unearthes.

Please sway and linger like the soil's thistles,
the yellow leaf's season, the flattened shadows.
O yes, our drums were carved by the sea,
its mother foam and Thunderbird.
Like the blue wind among blue willow,
the surf unites harvest dreams to stars,
deep currents, snipe and coot, starfish and black bass,
      footprints ingrained.

Fox woman, come dance with me,
let's find earth's beach, unravel yourself and tide,
let grass burn ocher, your hands be blue camas,
we'll turn as mischievous as Raven stealing light.
O I am best welcoming a friend.
So let's mingle with guest and ancestor,
Duckabush river and tamahnous, release the abalone
      yearnings, the eyeless flights.

SNOWY OWL NEAR OCEAN SHORES ❧

sits on a stump in an abandoned farmer's field,
a castaway from an arctic tundra storm.
Beyond the dunes cattails toss and bend as snappy
as the surf, rushing and crashing down the jetty.

His head glances round; his eyes, a deeper yellow
than the winter sun, seem to spot a mouse
crawl from a mud hole to bear grass-patch.
When an hour of wind and sleet passes and nothing
darts like the river underground, a North Pole
creature shows us how to last.

The wind ruffles his feathers from crown to claws
while he gazes at the salt-slick rain.
So when a double-rainbow arced the sky
we left him to his white refrain.

Glossary

The following words used in this collection may be unfamiliar to some readers. The definitions, supplied by the poet, relate to the words as they are used in the context of the poems.

Camas: A blue lily with edible bulbs which was a staple food for many of the Salishan tribes. The name is derived from a West Coast (Nootka) word meaning "sweet."

Cankpe Opi: The Lakota name for Wounded Knee, South Dakota, where a band of Lakota led by Big Foot were massacred by the 7th Calvary in 1891. Also the scene of armed confrontation between U.S. Marshals and members of the American Indian Movement in 1973.

Elwha: A river in the Klallam home country.

Ho-Had-Hun: The Nisqually name for what are now called the Olympic Mountains.

Ho-ho-kam: A Pima word meaning "those who have vanished," referring to the extinct civilization which flourished in southern Arizona, along the Gila River, from 500 to 1200 A.D. The Pimas are said to have descended from them.

Hoko: Another Klallam river.

Klallam: A Salishan tribe living on the Washington coast, along the Strait of Juan de Fuca. Their name means "strong people." The author is enrolled in this tribe, the N'huia-wulsh (Jamestown band).

Kwatee: The Changer of Quinault mythology.

Lach-ka-nim: (Prince of Wales): the seventh son of Chief Ste-tee-thlum of N'huia-wulsh (Jamestown). N'huia-wulsh translates as "village of white firs."

Leschi: An early chief of the Nisqually People, executed by the Washington territorial militia after leading an unsuccessful war to regain his tribe's ancestral homeland from the white settlers.

Longhouse: The traditional home of the tribes of the Northwest Coast. It was carved from red cedar and often housed extended families.

Memp-ch-ton: The Klallam name for Mount Olympus, in the heart of the Klallam country.

Moon of Dry Grass: Lummi tribe's name for August.

Nisqually: A Salishan tribe living near the southern end of Puget Sound.

Round Dance: is a traditional social dance among tribal people throughout North America. It is a friendship dance and is meant to break the ice.

Seatco: An evil spirit, or spirits, greatly feared by many of the Salishan tribes living along the Washington and Oregon coasts.

Skoaquik: The Pima name for present day Snaketown, Arizona. Skoaquik was once the central village of the Hohokam culture.

Snoqualmie: A Salishan tribe living in Western Washington. Their name means "people who came from the moon."

Tamahnous: A Klallam word that refers to what they consider a guardian spirit, often personified as courage.

Tillicum: The Chinook word for friend.

The poems in the "New Poems" section of this book were originally published in the following periodicals. The author and publisher wish to gratefully acknowledge permission to reprint:

The Chariton Review: "Snowy Owl Near Ocean Shores"
Contact II: "Four Mobiles After an Alexander Calder Retrospective"
Fine Madness: "Winter in New York"
The Greenfield Review: "Meditation on Visiting Hurricane Ridge," "Apology"
The Malahat Review: "The Waterfall Song," "The Reality of Autumn"
The New England Review: "The Passenger"
Paris/Atlantic: "Lines for Roethke Twenty Years after His Death"
Poetry Now: "Maggie"
Seattle Review: "At the International Poetry Festival," "Visiting My Son Marc at Port Angeles"
Shantih: "Summer Voices" under the title "Certain Voices of Summer"
Spindrift: "The Traveler" and "In the Age When Someone is Always Leaving"
The Village Voice: "The Musician"
Whetstone: "The Target"
Wicazo Sa Review: "Spring Currents" and "Round Dance"

Poems from the following out of print books are included in this volume:

After the Death of An Elder Klallam, Baleen Press, 1970; *Ascending Red Cedar Moon,* Harper & Row, Inc., 1974; *Digging Out the Roots,* Harper & Row, Inc., 1977; and *Songs for the Harvester of Dreams,* University of Washington Press, 1981.

"Apology," "Maggie," "The Traveler," "The Reality of Autumn," "The Art of Clay," "Lines for Roethke Twenty Years after His Death," and "Snowy Owl Near Ocean Shores" appeared in *Harper's Anthology of 20th Century Native American Poetry,* edited by Duane Niatum, Harper and Row, Inc., 1988.

I would like to thank my friends and fellow writers who gave the manuscript critical readings as it was revised and selected. They are: Nelson Bentley, Ramona Weeks, Joseph Bruchac III, Marjan van der A, Brian Swann, Jeff Smith, and, of course, my new editor and publisher, Jim Perlman.

Duane Niatum was born in 1938 in Seattle, Washington. A Native American of mixed descent, he is a member of the Klallam tribe, whose ancestral lands are on the Washington coast along the Strait of Juan de Fuca. His early life was spent in Washington, Oregon, California, and Alaska, and at age seventeen he enlisted in the Navy and spent two years in Japan. On his return he completed his undergraduate studies in English at the University of Washington. He later received his M.A. from the Johns Hopkins University in 1972. After attending the University of Michigan for three years, he returned to Seattle in late autumn of 1990 to finish a Ph.D. dissertation on contemporary Northwest Coast painting and sculpture.

His poetry, short stories, and essays, have been published in such magazines as *The Nation, Prairie Schooner, Northwest Review, The American Poetry Review,* and many other literary journals and anthologies. His previously published collections of poems are *After the Death of an Elder Klallam, Ascending Red Cedar Moon, Digging Out the Roots,* and *Songs for the Harvester of Dreams,* which won the National Book Award from the Before Columbus Foundation in 1982.

In 1973-74 he was editor of the Native American Authors series at Harper & Row, and in 1975 he served as the editor of *Carriers of the Dream Wheel,* the most widely read book of contemporary Native American poetry. In 1988 Harper & Row published a sequel to *Carriers of the Dream Wheel* entitled *Harper's Anthology of 20th Century Native American Poetry.*

His most recent teaching position was at the University of Washington. In June, 1983, he was invited to participate in Rotterdam's International Poetry Festival. His poems, stories and essays have been translated into twelve languages including Italian, Dutch, Russian, and French.